The Apple Pie Tree

BY **Zoe Hall**

ILLUSTRATED BY **Shari Halpern**

SCHOLASTIC INC.
New York Toronto London Auckland Sydney

For Maw and her mile-high apple pies.
— S.H.

ISBN 0-590-62383-4

Text copyright © 1996 by Zoe Hall.
Illustrations copyright © 1996 by Shari Halpern.
All rights reserved. Published by Scholastic Inc.

SCHOLASTIC and associated logos are trademarks and/or registered trademarks of Scholastic Inc.

50 49 48 47 46 45 44 43   16 17/0

Printed in the U.S.A.   40

Special thanks to A. Ellen Terpstra and the staff of the International Apple Institute, and Greg Butcher of the American Birding Association, for their expert advice about apples and robins. If you would like a list of educational materials about apples, you can contact the International Apple Institute, 6707 Old Dominion Drive, Suite 320, McLean, VA 22101.

The illustrations for this book were created using a painted and found-paper collage technique.
Design by Kristina Iulo and Kathleen Westray

M y sister and I have a tree that grows the best part of apple pie.

Can you guess what that is?

Apples!
And every year,
we watch our apple tree grow.

In winter, our apple tree
is brown and bare.

But in spring,
leaves grow
on every branch.

Look! Two robins
are building a nest
in our tree.

Tiny pink flower buds
appear on the branches.
The robins chirp loudly,
guarding their eggs.

Just when the flower buds open,

baby robins break through the eggshells.

Now our tree is covered with blossoms.
And the baby robins begin to grow feathers.

When breezes blow,
the petals fall to the ground.
Mama and Papa Robin
teach their little birds to fly.

Some days it rains,
and the wind blows hard.
But our apple tree is strong.
And the robins are safe
in the branches.

Small green apples grow
where the blossoms used to be.

Soon it is summer.
The apples get bigger and bigger.

The little robins have grown up.
But they visit every day.

The branches bend down low.
They are covered with
big, round apples.

Now it is autumn.
The apples are red and ready to be picked!
We fill our basket to the brim.

Mom and Dad help us
peel the apples, cut them up,
and pile them into a pie shell.
Then we sprinkle cinnamon
and sugar over the top.

Mom puts the pan in the oven.

At last, the pie is cooked
and ready to be eaten.

Our tree has grown an apple pie!
It smells so good!

And it tastes delicious!

There's nothing as good
as an apple pie
you grew yourself.

How bees help our apples grow:

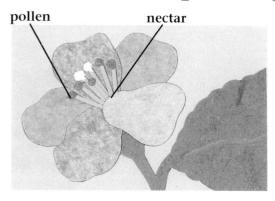

pollen nectar

pollen

1. Inside each flower are tiny stems, some tipped with yellow **pollen**, and some with sticky tops. **Nectar** deep inside smells sweet.

2. The bright petals and sweet nectar attract bees. **Pollen** collects on the bees' bodies.

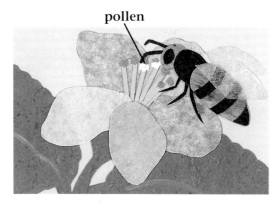

pollen

an apple begins to grow

3. As the bees fly from flower to flower, **pollen** clings to the sticky tops. This is called **pollination**.

4. The petals fall off, and the base of the flower begins to swell. This is the beginning of an **apple**.

This is how we make our apple pie!

1. **Make the pie crust:** Mix 2 cups all-purpose flour and 1 teaspoon salt in a large bowl. Cut up ⅔ cup butter into small pieces and mix in. Sprinkle ⅓ cup ice water on top and mix till the dough makes a loose ball. Cut in half. Roll out one half on a floured board to form a circle 12 inches across, ⅛ inch thick. Gently place in a 9-inch pie pan. Roll out remaining dough the same way, and cover with a towel.

2. **Fill the pie:** Peel 6 to 8 apples and cut them up, removing the centers. Put the slices into the pie pan. Sprinkle 1 teaspoon cinnamon and ½ cup sugar over the slices.

3. **Close the pie:** Place the second circle of dough over the apples. Pinch the edges together, and trim off the extra dough. Make small holes in the top.

4. **Bake** at 400° for 50 minutes. Serve and eat. Yum!